40 SIMPLE TO SEW FRENCH HOMESTYLE PROJECTS

French Country *chic*

LISE MEUNIER

D&C
David and Charles
www.rucraft.co.uk

4

9

45

87

119

141

144

CONTENTS

INTRODUCTION
4

THE WORKSHOP
9

THE SITTING ROOM
45

THE BEDROOM
87

PATTERNS
119

DIRECTORY
141

ACKNOWLEDGEMENTS
144

As a child, I was lulled to sleep by the sound of sewing machines, amid the feverish atmosphere of spring, when my grandmother's dining room would transform into a couture workshop.

I spent hours quietly hiding beneath the table, like a little mouse. I'd make up stories with scraps of cloth, creating families of buttons, yarn and thread in all the colours of the rainbow. Fascinated, I used to watch as magnificent knitwear took shape and shimmering outfits were made by deft hands. These were special moments that set me on the path to where I am today. Yet, it took time for me to begin my own sewing adventures.

When I first moved into a typical, small, dark Parisian apartment, I started to look for decorating solutions to make the rooms appear lighter and larger, to transform on a budget the few pieces of furniture given to me by my family, to use all the beautiful, vintage fabrics, lace and tassels I had amassed from second-hand markets and garage sales. And so I discovered 'shabby chic', a lovely mix of reclaimed furniture, beautiful materials and pretty objects for the creation of affordable antiques; so simple, yet so stylish. It was a question of getting stuck in, transforming, repainting and adapting what I had accumulated. Just what I love doing! And so I discovered the joy of creating my own home accents. I hope that, through this book, I can share with you my passion for decoration and sewing, by the making of simple, delicate objects.

I am dedicating this work to all the women from my childhood who inspired my creativity.

AS A CHILD, I WAS LULLED TO SLEEP BY THE SOUND OF SEWING MACHINES

THE WORKSHOP

APRON

10

SEAT PAD

14

COVERED BOXES

16

COTTON REEL HOLDER

20

PENCIL CASE

22

NEEDLE ROLL

24

WOOL BASKET

26

KEY HOLDER

30

PIN CUSHION

32

DRAWSTRING BAG

34

BLACKBOARD

38

JAR LABELS

40

APRON

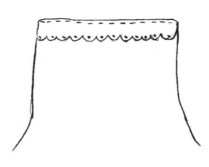

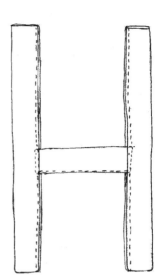

1 m (40 in) of woollen cloth dyed blue, 140 cm (55 in) wide
40 x 25 cm (15⅝ x 10 in) of printed fabric for the pocket and the button
70 cm (27½ in) of embroidered edging from a piece of vintage clothing or pillowcase
1 self-cover button, 23mm (⅛ in) in diameter
pattern paper
matching thread
pins

---

1. Draw the pattern by referring to the apron diagram in the Patterns section and cut out. (Note, all seam allowances are included.) Fold the fabric in half and pin the half apron, bar and strap pattern pieces on top, placing the half-apron piece on the fold. Cut out.

2. At the armholes, cut notches 1.5 cm (⅝ in) into the curves. To hem, make a double turn-up totalling 3 cm (1⅛ in) and stitch. To hem the top of the apron, along the sides and at the bottom, make an initial turn-up 1 cm (⅜ in) from the edge then a second 3 cm (1⅛ in) turn-up, and stitch along the edge of the fabric.

3. Make a 5 mm (¼ in) turn-up around each strap and press flat. Fold the straps in half along the length. Fold the bar in the same way, then slip it between the two straps approx. 35 cm (13¾ in) from the top, to form an "H" (see diagram, top right). Stitch along each strap.

4. Pin the top of the straps under the bib of the apron, at each end. Stitch in the shape of a rectangle, then stitch a cross in the rectangle. Stitch the straps in place in the same way on the back of the apron, 8 cm (3⅛ in) from each edge. Pin a length of embroidered edging at the top of the bib and stitch.

5. Cut out the rectangle for the pocket from the printed fabric. Pin the embroidered edging to the top of the pocket, right side to wrong side; stitch 5 mm (¼ in) from the edge, then turn back onto the right side and press flat. Hem the sides and bottom of the pocket with a 1 cm (⅜ in) turn-up; remove excess fabric at the corners, then press flat. Pin the pocket centrally onto the front of the apron and stitch in place.

6. Cover the button in printed fabric and sew onto the right side of the apron back. To make the buttonhole on the left side, cut out a horizontal slit 2 cm (¾ in) long and sew around with buttonhole stitch.

SEAT PAD

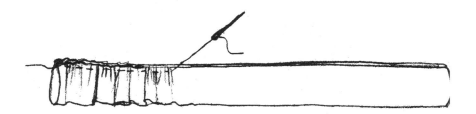

vintage woollen cloth
white thread
pins

1.   Cut a square the size of the seat of the chair from the woollen cloth, allowing 1 cm (⅜ in) extra on each side. Also cut a 9 cm (3½ in) wide strip that is eight times the length of one side.

2.   Make a double hem 1 cm (⅜ in) at the short ends and along one of the long sides of the fabric strip. Work a line of long running (gathering) stitches along the unhemmed side.

3.   Gather the fabric and pin it around the fabric square, right sides facing. Stitch by machine 1 cm (⅜ in) away from the edge; press the seams open.

COVERED BOXES

DMC

FIL AU TA…

BRODER à la CROIX
C·B   116   COULEUR
SOLIDE   20
12 Echeveaux de 32 Mètr.

36

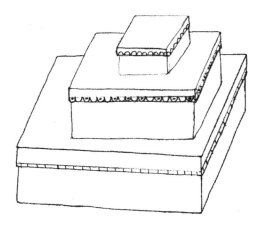

boxes in different sizes
floral fabrics
liquid vinyl adhesive
braid
paint brush

---

1.   If your box is covered with a print that will show through the fabric, you will need to paint it white first. Leave to dry.

2.   Measure the sides of the box and cut a strip of fabric to the same dimensions allowing 1 cm (⅜ in) for the join. Coat the box with adhesive and glue the fabric on top, overlapping it at the join.

3.   Cut out a piece of fabric in the dimensions of the lid (edges + top). Coat the lid with adhesive and glue the fabric on top, pinching the fabric at the corners and turning it back on one side. Leave to dry.

4.   Glue a piece of braid around the edge of the lid. Coat the whole of the surface of the fabric with adhesive to varnish.

5.   You can use paper to cover your boxes in the same way. One idea is to photocopy fabrics, but make sure you iron them well first.

COTTON REEL HOLDER

recycled rectangular frame
piece of MDF 5 mm (¼ in) thick to fit the internal dimensions of the frame
fine card in the same dimensions as the piece of MDF
rectangle of fabric slightly larger than the piece of MDF
9 carpenter's nails, 7 cm (2¾ in) in size
several strips of lace the width of the fabric
fabric adhesive
paint brush

1. Iron the fabric and glue it onto the piece of MDF folding it over to the back. Also glue on the lace.

2. Mark the position of the nails, then attach them at a slight angle using a little wedge to ensure the same incline for each.

3. Place the piece of MDF into the frame and glue the card onto the reverse.

PENCIL CASE

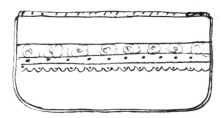

2 rectangles of different printed fabrics, 12 x 21 cm (4¾ x 8¼ in)
2 rectangles of white cotton, (4¾ x 8¼ in)
3 lace ribbons, 21 cm (8¼ in)
37 cm (14½ in) of white piping
white zip fastener, 18 cm (7 in)
pattern paper
matching thread
pins

1.   Photocopy the pencil case pattern (see Patterns) onto pattern paper and cut out. Pin to the reverse of the printed fabrics and white cotton rectangles. Cut out 1 cm (⅜ in) from the side and bottom edges and 1.5 cm (⅝ in) from the edge along the top opening.

2.   Position the lace strips side by side across one piece of the printed fabric, and sew them on by hand or machine.

3.   Place the two pieces of printed fabric on top of each other, right sides facing. Sandwich the piping between the two from one side of the opening to the other and pin in place. Machine stitch 1 cm (⅜ in) away from the edge. Cut notches into the curves.

4.   Open the zip fastener and pin each part to either side of the opening, on the reverse of the fabric. Stitch 1 cm (⅜ in) away from the edge, using the special zipper foot on the sewing machine. Otherwise, sew with a traditional foot and finish by hand. Turn out the pencil case to the right side.

5.   Place the two white cotton pieces on top of each other and stitch from one side of the opening to the other with a 1 cm (⅜ in) seam allowance. Cut notches into the curves, and if necessary trim the fabric closer to the seam. Fold over 1 cm (⅜ in) to the reverse of the lining, right around the opening.

6.   Slip the lining into the pencil case and sew the top in place by hand, using slip stitch.

NEEDLE ROLL

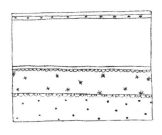
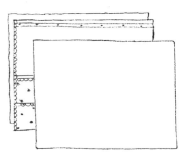

2 rectangles of woollen/linen mix cloth, 44 x 42 cm (17¼ x 16½ in)
44 x 42 cm (17¼ x 16½ in) of fleece
44 x 22 cm (17¼ x 8⅝ in) and 110 x 10 cm (43⅛ x 4 in) of floral fabric
44 x 12 cm (17¼ x 4¾ in) of floral fabric in another print
4 strips of different lace and of scalloped edging, 44 cm (17¼ in)
2 strips of lace, 42 cm (16½ in)
white thread
pins

1.   Sew a strip of lace onto each of the two woollen/linen rectangles, 4 cm (1½ in) from the top. Take the 44 cm (17¼ in) wide rectangles of floral fabric and machine stitch a double turn-up 1 cm (⅜ in) high along one long edge of each. Sew strips of lace onto the stitches of the hems, on the right side.

2.   Pin the floral fabrics, with right sides facing up, to the bottom of a piece of woollen/linen cloth, matching up the raw edges (see diagram, top). Pin the fleece to the reverse.

3.   Pin a strip of lace along each side of the fabric sandwich, lining up the edges and with the right sides facing you. Place the second rectangle of woollen/linen cloth on top, right sides facing, and stitch with a 1 cm (⅜ in) seam allowance, leaving an opening of around 12 cm (4¾ in). Trim the excess fabric at the corners and turn right side out. Close the opening using slip stitch and press.

4.   Make the tie by folding in half the floral fabric 110 cm (43⅛ in) strip, lengthways, right sides facing. Stitch with a 1 cm (⅜ in) seam allowance, leaving an opening in the middle for turning out. Trim excess fabric at the corners, turn out, press, and close the opening.

5.   Pin the tie strip centrally to the back of the needle roll, so that the ends are the same length on each side. Stitch three vertical seams 10.5 cm (4¼ in) apart to make the pockets, catching the ribbon in the seam.

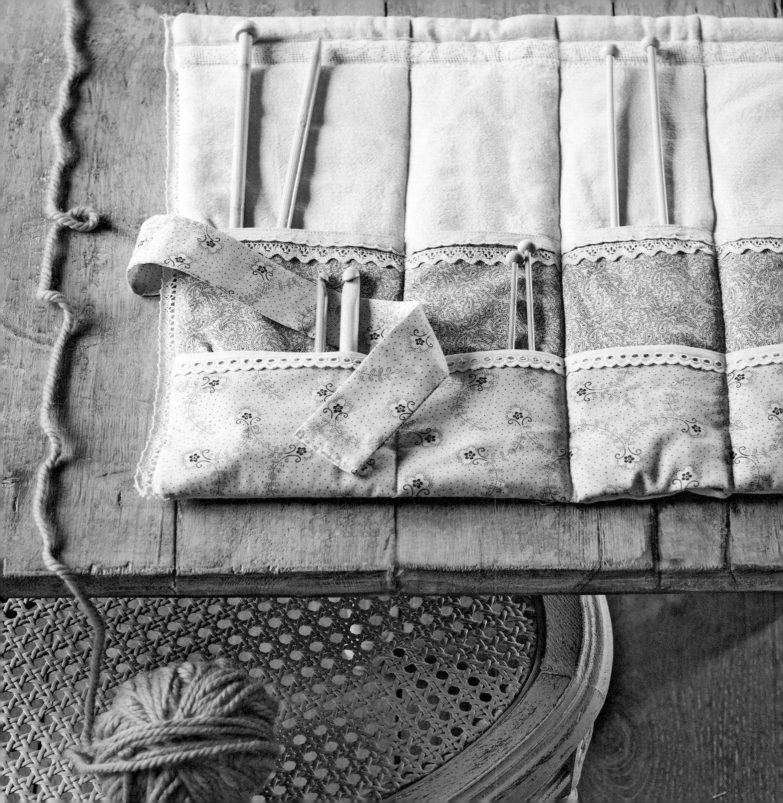

WOOL BASKET

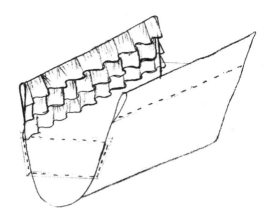

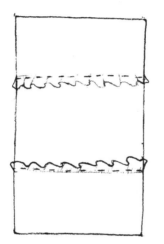

46 x 76 cm (18 x 30 in) of white linen
2 rectangles of white linen, 28 x 18 cm (11 x 7 in)
6 strips of white linen, 90 x 8 cm (35¼ x 3⅛ in)
4 strips of white linen, 25 x 3 cm (9⅞ x 1⅛ in)
white thread
pins

1. Press a 1 cm (⅜ in) fold along one long side of one of the 90 cm (35¼ in) strips, and stitch a double turn-up of 1 cm (⅜ in) by machine on the other long side. Work a line of long running (gathering) stitches along the fold and gather to make a 42 cm (16½ in) frill. Repeat for the other five strips.

2. Hem the long edges of the large linen rectangle with a double turn-up 1 cm (⅜ in) high. Turn over a 3 cm (1⅛ in) hem along the short edges on the reverse and stitch at the edge.

3. Pin the frills to either end of the rectangle, parallel to the width. The first frill is pinned 9 cm (3½ in) from the edge (see diagram, top left), the second, which overlaps the first, 6 cm (2⅜ in) from the edge and the third 3 cm (1⅛ in) from the edge. Each frill overlaps the other by 2 cm (¾ in). Stitch the frills.

4. Fold over the edge at the top of the last frill at either end for a 3 cm (1⅛ in) turn-up. Stitch this turn-up along the edge, to make casings (for the basket holder's poles), taking care not to catch the frill in the seam.

5. Referring to the knitting basket diagram in the Patterns section, make a side bar pattern and use to cut out two trapezium shapes onto the small rectangles of linen. Press a 1 cm (⅜ in) double turn-up on each side of the side bars. Trim excess fabric at the corners and stitch.

6. Fold the frilled rectangle in half, right sides facing, and pin the sides bars (with the longest edge at the top) 10 cm (4 in) from the top, with the right side of the side bars to the wrong side of the rectangle. Stitch 5 mm (¼ in) from the edges and turn out.

7. Press a 5 mm (¼ in) fold around the remaining linen strips. Fold in half lengthways, wrong sides facing, and stitch close to the edge. Fold the strips in half and sew, at the fold, to the sides of the basket, 9 cm (3½ in) from the top.

8. Iron the finished piece and attach it to the holder. Tie the four ties onto the legs of the basket holder.

KEY HOLDER

self-hardening modelling clay, white
acrylic paint, cream
satin varnish
fine linen string
tracing paper
wooden skewer
craft knife
rolling pin
fine paint brush
large needle

1. Trace and cut out the key holder patterns (see Patterns).

2. Work the clay and roll out to around 5 mm (¼ in) thick.

3. Place the patterns on the clay and cut around using the craft knife. Pierce a hole in each shape with the skewer and draw on details as you wish with the tip of the needle. Smooth out any errors by moistening slightly, then leave to dry.

4. Paint and varnish. Pass a piece of string through each hole to attach the keys.

PIN CUSHION

candlestick (wooden, copper or brass)
undercoat, white
paint, blue
foam board 3mm (⅛ in) thick
scrap of fabric
lace
wadding (batting)
matching thread
paint brush
strong adhesive
pair of compasses

1.   Paint the candlestick with the undercoat, leave to dry then paint blue. Leave to dry thoroughly.

2.   Cut out a circle from the foam board to the required diameter. Glue onto the candlestick.

3.   Cut out a circle of fabric, where the diameter equals twice that of the foam board circle. Work two lines of long running (gathering) stitches around the edge of the circle.

4.   Place a ball of wadding (batting) on the foam board, place the fabric on top and gather by pulling up the thread. Tighten the fabric around the candlestick and tie the thread firmly.

5.   Sew some lace all around the edges of the pin cushion, level with the foam board.

DRAWSTRING BAG

FOR THE STRIPED BAG

38 x 26 cm (15 x 10⅛ in) of striped fabric

38 x 12 cm (15 x 4¾ in) of white woollen cloth

9 x 7 cm (3½ x 2¾ in) of printed fabric

an embroidered monogram cut in an oval

19 cm (7½ in) of lace

50 cm (20 in) of linen string

white and matching thread

pins

---

1.   Press over 1 cm (⅜ in) all the way around the printed fabric. Hem the monogram and sew it in the middle of the printed fabric. Sew the monogrammed rectangle onto the striped fabric, 3 cm (1⅛ in) from the bottom and 2 cm (¾ in) from the right side.

2.   Oversew the top of the striped fabric and one long side of the white fabric strip. Pin together the oversewn edges, right sides facing. Machine stitch 1 cm (⅜ in) away from the edge and press the seam open. Oversew, then fold this rectangle in half, right sides facing, to form a rectangle 36 x 19 cm (14⅛ x 7½ in). Sandwich the strip of lace between the fabric, at the bottom of the bag, so that the edge of the lace is caught in the seam; pin.

3.   Stitch the bottom and the side of the bag 1 cm (⅜ in) away from the edge, leaving an opening of 1 cm (⅜ in) 5 cm (2 in) from the top. Fold the white fabric down by 1 cm (⅜ in), wrong sides facing, then fold down by 6 cm (2⅜ in), and stitch right around the opening, close to the edge. Then make a second row of stitching, 1 cm (⅜ in) above. Trim excess fabric at the corners. Turn out the bag and thread a piece of linen string through the drawstring channel using a safety pin. Make other bags using the same principle.

BLACKBOARD

piece of MDF 60 x 40 cm (23½ x 15⅝ in), 1 cm (⅜ in) thick
blackboard paint
30 cm (12 in) of linen string
jig-saw
drill with a fine, wood bit
fine sandpaper
small roller or wide, flat paint brush
narrow, flat paint brush

1. Enlarge the blackboard pattern by 200% (see Patterns). Cut out and transfer onto the piece of MDF.

2. Cut out very carefully using the jig-saw following the outline of the pattern.

3. Pierce a hole at the top of the MDF, centred. Sand the edges using the sandpaper and clean off the dust.

4. Paint the MDF with blackboard paint using the roller (or wide paint brush) and the edges using the narrow paint brush. Leave to dry for the required time. Apply a second coat and leave to dry again.

5. Slip a little piece of ribbon through the hole to hang up the blackboard.

JAR LABELS

scraps of different ribbons and braid
scraps of white fabric, patterned fabric and embroidered monograms
letter stamps
acrylic paint
small buttons
matching thread
pins

1. Cut out a rectangle of white cotton 7 x 5 cm (2¾ x 2 in) and sew a 5 mm (¼ in) hem around the edges. Press flat.

2. Stamp/embroider your chosen word onto the label. Pin and sew the decorated label to the middle of the ribbons.

3. Position the label on the front of the jar, wrap the ribbons around to the back and sew in place.

4. Get creative and make other labels using the same principle using the fabrics, ribbons and embellishments you have gathered together.

THE SITTING ROOM

CHAIR COVER
46

FABRIC FRUIT & VEGETABLES
48

DISPLAY BOARD
52

LAMP SHADE
54

PLANT POT COVERS
56

LARGE TOTE
60

BREAD BASKET
62

NOTEBOOK COVERS
64

TABLECLOTH & NAPKINS
68

HEART CUSHION
72

HANGING ORNAMENT
74

ARMCHAIR RENOVATION
76

RECTANGULAR CUSHION
78

FLOOR CUSHION
80

PLASTER STATUE
82

CHAIR COVER

80 x 100 cm (31⅜ x 39¼ in) of vintage, dyed woollen cloth
50 cm (20 in) of printed fabric
matching thread
pins

1.   Measure the chair starting with the back legs, then the chair back (back and front), the seat and finally the front legs. Also measure the width of the chair (see Patterns). Cut out a long strip of fabric to these measurements, adding an extra 2 cm (¾ in) all around for the seams. If your fabric is not long enough, cut in several pieces and join together, pressing open the seams.

2.   Measure the sides of the chair (height of the legs x depth of the seat) adding 2 cm (¾ in) for the seams all around. Cut out two pieces from the woollen cloth fabric to these measurements.

3.   Stitch a double hem right around the long strip of fabric. For the sides, stitch a double hem on the long sides and at the bottom.

4.   Position the cover on the chair and pin the sides. Remove the cover, stitch the sides, right sides facing, and press open the seams.

5.   Draw a large heart onto the printed fabric and cut around the outline. Pin to the centre of the chair back and stitch around the edges with satin stitch.

6.   To make the ties, cut out 12 strips 32.5 x 2.5 cm (12½ x 1 in) from the printed fabric. Fold over the edges by 3mm (⅛ in), fold in half, wrong sides together, along the length, and machine stitch to close.

7.   Pin the ties to the reverse of the cover, in the middle of the height of the legs and at the base of the chair back, ensuring that they match up. Sew firmly in place.

FABRIC FRUIT
& VEGETABLES

FOR THE PEAR
20 cm (8 in) of calico (muslin)
4 cm (1½ in) of wire
wadding (batting)
stranded cotton (floss), ecru
white thread
pins

1.   Make a template of the pear and pear leaf (see Patterns) and use to mark the three pears and the two pear leaves onto the fabric. Cut out adding 5 mm (¼ in) for the seams. Also cut a rectangle 4 x 1 cm (1½ x ⅜ in).

2.   Pin the three pieces of fabric for the pear, right sides facing and lining up the edges. Machine stitch close to the edge, leaving a tiny opening at the top. Leave an opening of a few centimetres (about an inch) at the bottom of one of the seams. Cut notches into the curves, turn right side out. Fill with wadding (batting) and close the bottom opening by hand.

3.   Sew the two parts of the leaf in the same way, right sides facing, and turn right side out through the opening. Close using slip stitch. Embroider the central vein using running stitch, with two strands of the embroidery thread.

4.   To make the stem, take the calico (muslin) rectangle and fold over along the long edges a little way. Then fold the fabric in half, lengthways, wrong sides facing. Stitch the length close to the edge to close the stem and slip the wire inside. Push one end of the stem into the tiny opening at the top of the pear. Secure in place with a few stitches. Sew the base of the leaf onto the stem.

FOR THE PUMPKIN
100 x 15 cm (39¼ x 5¾ in) calico (muslin)
9 cm (3½ in) of wire
wadding (batting)
stranded cotton (floss), ecru
white thread
pins

---

1.   Cut a strip from the calico (muslin) 80 x 15 cm (31⅜ x 5¾ in) and fold in half to form a rectangle 40 x 15 cm (15⅝ x 5¾ in). Machine stitch along the short edge, with a 1 cm (⅜ in) seam allowance, to close into a circle. Press the seam open and turn out. Work a line of long running (gathering) stitches around the top and bottom edges. Pull up the thread at the bottom and tie firmly to close. Fill tightly with wadding (batting) and gather at the top without tying the thread.

2.   Use the pumpkin leaf template (see Patterns) to cut two leaves from the calico (muslin), adding a 3mm (⅛ in) seam allowance. Pin the two pieces of the leaf, right sides facing, and stitch 3mm (⅛ in) from the edge all around, leaving an opening of 3 cm (1⅛ in). Cut notches into the curves, turn out and close the opening by hand. Embroider the veins using running stitch, with two strands of the embroidery thread.

3.   Cut out a calico (muslin) strip 10 x 3 cm (4 x 1⅛ in) and fold over the edges by 5 mm (¼ in) all around. Position the wire in the middle and fold the strip in half, wrong sides facing, and stitch.

4.   Fold the remaining fabric in half, mark the pumpkin stem on top and cut the fabric adding a 3mm (⅛ in) seam allowance. Place the two pieces right sides facing, stitch leaving an opening, cut notches and turn out (use a knitting needle to help you turn out the very end). Fill with wadding (batting) and close by hand. Sew the stem onto the back of the leaf. Slip the other end of the stem into the pumpkin. Secure in place with a few stitches and close the opening tying the gathering thread firmly.

5.   With a long length of stranded cotton (floss), stitch at the base of the pumpkin and bring the needle out level with the stem, then stitch again from below at the centre. Repeat this process several times to define the segments of the pumpkin.

FOR THE CAULIFLOWER

45 x 20 cm (17⅝ x 8 in) of calico (muslin)

40 x 20 cm (15⅝ x 8 in) of white cotton
wadding (batting)

stranded cotton (floss), ecru

white thread

pins

1. Fold the calico (muslin) in half to give you a rectangle measuring 45 x 10 cm (17⅝ x 4 in). Make a template of the cauliflower leaf (see Patterns) and use to mark the cauliflower leaf five times onto the fabric. Cut out the fabric adding a 3mm (⅛ in) seam allowance.

2. To make the five leaves, pin the pieces two by two, right sides facing, and stitch with a 3mm (⅛ in) seam allowance, leaving an opening of 3 cm (1⅛ in). Cut notches into the curves, turn out and close the openings by hand. Embroider the edge and a central vein using running stitch, with two strands of embroidery thread.

3. Cut a circle 13 cm (5in) in diameter from the white fabric and 12 circles 5 cm (2 in) in diameter. Work a line of long running (gathering) stitches around each circle, place some wadding (batting) in the middle and draw up the thread to close.

4. Sew the little balls on top of the large ball, making them overlap slightly. Pin the leaves all around, right up underneath the cauliflower, making them overlap by 1 to 2 cm (⅜ to ¾ in). Sew using blind stitch.

DISPLAY BOARD

vintage frame
foam board 4 mm (⁵⁄₃₂ in) thick, cut to the size of the inside of the frame
fleece roll, cut to the size of the inside of the frame
printed fabric, cut to the size of the outside of the frame
acrylic paint, blue and white
paint brush
2 strips of lace, the width of the frame
pins
sandpaper, fine and medium grain

1.   Paint the frame with two coats of blue paint and leave to dry thoroughly. Then paint white and leave to dry thoroughly again. Sand to remove the white paint in places so that the blue paint shows through.

2.   Trace the inside edge of the frame onto the foam board and cut out. Place the fleece onto the foam board, then place the fabric on top. Fold the fabric over the edge of the foam board and pin all the way around, to hold it tightly. Place the strips of lace horizontally across the top of the fabric and pin in the same way.

3.   Place the foam board in the frame. If necessary, hold it in place at the back with some tacks.

LAMP SHADE

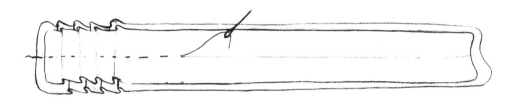

white cotton lamp shade
6 cm (2⅜ in) of white cotton x 2 times the circumference of the bottom of the lamp shade
4 cm (½ in) of white cotton x 2 times the circumference of the bottom of the lamp shade
white thread
pins

1.   Fold the strips of fabric in half, lengthways, and press to mark the folds.

2.   Pin the 4 cm (1½ in) strip onto the 6 cm (2⅜ in) strip lining up the two folds.

3.   Work a line of long running (gathering) stitches and gather up to fit around the bottom of the lamp shade.

4.   Pin on the frill lining up the gathering thread with the edge of the lamp shade. Sew the frill by hand above the gathering thread.

PLANT POT COVERS

printed fabric
ribbons, lace, braid
fabric adhesive
paint brush
matching thread
pins

1.   Measure a jar or bottle and cut a strip of fabric to these dimensions allowing 1 cm (⅜ in) extra on each side. Press under the top and bottom edges by 1 cm (⅜ in).

2.   Pin pieces of lace, ribbons and braid along the top and bottom edges as desired. Machine stitch in place or use fabric adhesive to secure. You could also add a button, some beads or any other decoration that appeals.

3.   Fold the cover in half, right sides facing, and stitch together with a 1 cm (⅜ in) seam allowance.

4.   Press the seam open, turn right side out and press again. Slip the cover over the jar/bottle.

LARGE TOTE

2 rectangles of vintage woollen cloth, 98 x 42 cm (38½ x 16½ in)

4 rectangles of vintage woollen cloth, 22 x 38 cm (8⅝ x 15in)

98 x 42 cm (38½ x 16½ in) of thick double-sided iron-on interfacing

2 rectangles of thick double-sided iron-on interfacing, 22 x 38 cm (8⅝ x 15in)

3 strips of different printed fabrics, 66 x 22 cm (30 x 8⅝ in), 54 x 18 cm (21¼ x 7 in) and 40 x 12 cm (15⅝ x 4¾ in)

2 strips of vintage woollen cloth, 34 x 6 cm (13⅜ x 2⅜ in)

2 strips of printed fabric cut on the bias, 100 x 4 cm (39¼ x 1½ in), for the sides

1 strip of printed fabric cut on the bias, 130 x 4 cm (51 x 1½ in), for the edge

3 large self-cover buttons

scraps of fabric

matching thread

pins

1.   To make the decorations, fold the strips of printed fabric in half, right sides facing, and machine stitch with a 1 cm (⅜ in) seam allowance to close up into a circle; press open the seams.

2.   Fold the circles in half, wrong sides facing, and work a line of long running (gathering) stitches along the edge of the open side, catching in the two thicknesses of fabric. Gather and finish off the thread to make each decoration. Sew the decorations onto one of the large woollen cloth rectangles, so that they overlap.

3.   Join the decorated woollen cloth rectangle to the undecorated woollen cloth rectangle by sandwiching the iron-on interfacing between the two. Make the bag sides in the same way.

4.   Pin the sides onto the bag, lining up the edges, wrong sides facing, and stitch with a 1 cm (⅜ in) seam allowance.

5.   Fold the strips of bias binding in half, wrong sides facing, and press. Open out and fold in each side to the centre, and press again.

6.   Pin the folded bias binding over the side seams and stitch. Edge the top of the bag in the same way.

7.   To make the handles, fold the strips of vintage woollen cloth in half and stitch along the length 1 cm (⅜ in) away from the edges. Turn them out with the help of a safety pin (pin the pin onto one end of a strip and slip it inside and bring it out the other side) and pin them inside the bag, 16 cm (6¼ in) from each side. Sew firmly.

8.   Cover the buttons with the fabric scraps and sew in the centre of each decoration.

BREAD BASKET

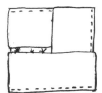

12 rectangles 22 x 12 cm (8⅝ x 4¾ in): 4 hemp cloth, 4 different printed fabrics and 4 iron-on interfacing
3 squares 22 x 22 cm (8⅝ x 8⅝ in): 1 hemp cloth, 1 printed cotton and 1 iron-on interfacing
4 strips 20 x 5 cm (8 x 2 in): 2 printed cotton and 2 iron-on interfacing
90 cm (35¼ in) of lace or scalloped edging
matching thread
pins

1. Line all the printed fabrics with the iron-on interfacing by ironing onto the reverse without using steam.

2. To make the outer layer, pin a printed rectangle onto the printed square, right sides facing and lining up the edges, and stitch with a 1 cm (⅜ in) seam allowance. Repeat for the remaining three sides (see diagram, left). Press open the seams. Lift up the sides; pin the sides to each other at each corner, with rightsides facing and lining up the edges, and stitch with a 1 cm (⅜ in) seam allowance. Trim off excess fabric at the corners.

3. To make the lining, repeat step 2 with the hemp square (base) and rectangles (sides).

4. To make the handles, fold the 20 x 5 cm (8 x 2 in) strips, right sides facing, lengthways. Stitch with a 5 mm (¼ in) seam allowance, leaving a small gap for turning through. Turn right side out, close the seam and press.

5. Open out the printed fabric basket and pin the handles onto the sides, on the right side of the printed fabric 5 cm (2 in) from each corner and with the handle pointing downwards.

6. Pin the two baskets to each other, right sides facing. Stitch with a 1 cm (⅜ in) seam allowance, leaving an opening of around 8 cm (3⅛ in) and catching in the ends of the handles in the seam.

7. Turn right side out through the opening. Push the hemp lining into the basket ensuring that the corners line up, then close the opening using slip stitch. Pin the lace all around the outer edge and sew it on using blind stitch.

NOTEBOOK COVERS

 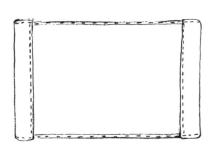

notebook
white woollen cloth
printed fabric
fine iron-on interfacing
fabric adhesive
paint brush
matching thread

1.   Cut a piece from the woollen cloth the size of both sides of the notebook, allowing an extra 1 cm (⅜ in) at the top and the bottom and 6 cm (2⅜ in) at each side. Fold over a 1 cm (⅜ in) hem all around, press flat and machine stitch (see diagram, top left). Fold over another 5 cm (2 in) on each side to make the flaps and stitch at the top and bottom, close to the edge (see diagram, top right).

2.   Line the printed fabrics with iron-on interfacing. For the kitchen notebook covers use the fork and spoon templates (see Patterns and reduce as necessary to fit your book cover) to mark their outlines onto the back of the printed fabric. Cut out and glue onto the cover of the notebook. Slip the notebook inside.

3.   To further decorate your notebook covers, sew on strips of lace and braid and tie them shut using ribbons.

TABLECLOTH & NAPKINS

FOR THE TABLECLOTH
2.4 x 1.5 m (94½ x 60 in) of linen fabric
a dozen remnants of fabric in shades of blue: plain, coloured, printed, etc.
pair of compasses
matching thread
pins

1. Press a double turn-up of 2 cm (¾ in) all around the tablecloth; machine stitch.

2. On the reverse of the printed fabrics, draw approx. 30 circles of different diameters, from 6 to 14 cm (2⅜ to 5½ in). Cut out 1 cm (⅜ in) away from the marked outlines, and cut notches all around.

3. Fold over the notched fabric to the reverse and press.

4. Scatter the circles over the tablecloth taking inspiration from the circle placement diagram (see Patterns): start at the centre and make them overlap slightly; as you work out to the edges, space them further and further apart.

5. Sew on the fabric circles using slip stitch, starting with those lying underneath.

FOR EACH NAPKIN
40 x 40 cm (15⅝ x 15⅝ in) linen fabric
scraps of printed fabrics used for the tablecloth
pair of compasses
matching thread
pins

1. Press a double turn-up of 2 cm (¾ in) all around the napkin. Machine stitch.

2. Make the circles as for the tablecloth and sew one or two circles onto each napkin.

HEART CUSHION

2 squares 40 x 40 cm (15⅝ x 15⅝ in) of white cotton
1 square 40 x 40 cm (15⅝ x 15⅝ in) of spotted fabric
2 rectangles 40 x 25 cm (15⅝ x 9⅞ in) of spotted fabric
wadding (batting)
matching thread
pins

1.   To make the cushion pad, place the two squares of white cotton on top of each other, right sides facing, and pin together. Draw a heart, cut out and then transfer its outline onto the fabric. Cut out 1 cm (⅜ in) away from the outline.

2.   Machine stitch the heart pieces together with a 1 cm (⅜ in) seam allowance, leaving an opening of around 12 cm (4¾ in). Cut notches into the curves and at the tip of the heart, and trim off the excess fabric. Turn out the cover to the right side, fill with wadding (batting) and close the opening using slip stitch.

3.   To make the cushion cover, transfer the heart template onto the reverse of the spotted square and cut out 1 cm (⅜ in) from the line.

4.   Stitch a double turn-up of 1 cm (⅜ in) on one of the long edges of each spotted fabric rectangle. Use the two rectangles to make a square 40 x 40 cm (15⅝ x 15⅝in), placing the hemmed sides on top of each other, right side to wrong side. Pin and transfer the heart template onto the reverse and cut out 1 cm (⅜ in) from the line.

5.   Pin the two spotted fabric hearts together, right sides facing. Stitch on the line, cut some notches and turn right side out. Press. Slip the cushion pad into the cover.

HANGING ORNAMENT

self-hardening modelling clay, white
2.5 m (98½ in) of fine, strong linen string
tracing paper
rolling pin
craft knife
wooden skewer

1.   Trace the bird template (see Patterns) and cut out.

2.   Work a piece of clay and roll out to a thickness of around 3mm (⅛ in).

3.   Place the bird template on the clay and run the craft knife around the edges to cut out. Pierce a hole in the tail with the skewer. Smooth the edges by moistening them slightly and leave to dry.

4.   Make beads in different diameters as follows: 10 beads 1 cm (⅜ in) in diameter, 100 beads 1.5 cm (⅝ in) in diameter and 40 beads 2 cm (¾ in) in diameter. Pierce with the skewer, smooth with water, and use the skewer to create patterns on some of them. Leave to dry thoroughly.

5.   Fold the string in half, slip the loop into the hole in the bird's tail, then pass the two ends through the loop and pull to attach the bird.

6.   Thread the 10 small beads onto the two strands, then separate the two strands. Thread 50 medium beads and 20 large beads onto each side. Tie firmly to close, then slip the two ends of the string into the beads on each side.

ARMCHAIR RENOVATION

armchair
fine sandpaper
acrylic paint, matt blue and white
striped fabric for the seat
floral fabric for the chair back
upholstery tacks
scraps of fabric for the flowers and the buttons
50 cm (20 in) of fine iron-on interfacing
2 self-cover buttons
braid
matching thread
pins
fabric adhesive
paint brush for the paint
paint brush for the adhesive

1.   Lightly sand the wood parts of the armchair, so that the paint will adhere, and wipe clean. Paint with two coats of blue paint, leaving to dry between each coat. Then apply two coats of white paint. After drying for 24 hours, lightly sand the edges and the raised areas so that the blue paint shows through. Wipe clean.

2.   Make a paper template of the shape of the chair back and the seat and transfer onto the reverse of the fabrics. Cut out.

3.   Line the scraps of fabric with iron-on interfacing. Photocopy the flower templates (see Patterns), cut out from card and draw around their outline onto the iron-on interfacing. Cut out on the marked lines. Position the flowers on the chair back fabric overlapping several of them, starting with the largest flowers on the bottom and finishing with the smallest on top, securing each flower as you go with slip stitch. Cover the buttons with fabric and sew at the centre of each flower.

4.   Position the fabric for the seat and the chair back on the armchair and tack all around in the wood, stretching it out well. Glue on the braid to hide the tacks.

RECTANGULAR CUSHION

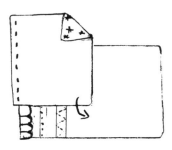 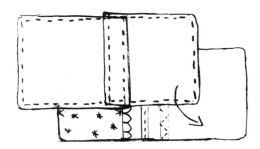

20 x 25 cm (8 x 9⅞ in)of floral cotton

28 x 25 cm (11 x 9⅞ in) of cotton in a different print

2 pieces 33 x 25 cm (13 x 9⅞ in) of off-white woollen cloth

25 cm (9⅞ in) of lace

25 cm (9⅞ in) of fine braid

25 cm (9⅞ in) of broderie anglaise

1 cushion pad, 23 x 43 cm (9 x 17 in)

matching thread

pins

---

1.   Place the two rectangles of printed fabric right sides facing, lining up the 25 cm (9⅞ in) widths. Slip the broderie anglaise between the two fabrics (see diagram, top left) and stitch with a 1 cm (⅜ in) seam allowance. Press the seam open. Stitch the strips of lace and braid onto the right side of the large, printed rectangle, so that they are parallel to the scalloped edging of the broderie anglaise.

2.   For the back of the cushion, stitch a double hem of 3 cm (1⅛ in) on one of the short sides of the woollen cloth rectangles, on the reverse. Place these two rectangles on the front of the cushion, right sides facing, overlapping the hemmed sides by approx. 8 cm (3⅛ in) so that the edges of the front and back align (see diagram, top right).

3.   Stitch all around with a 1 cm (⅜ in) seam allowance. Trim the excess fabric at the corners. Turn out the cover, iron and slip the cushion pad inside.

FLOOR CUSHION

 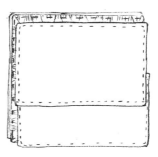

large, well-filled, square cushion pad, 63 x 63 cm (24¾ x 24¾in)
65 cm x 65 cm (25½ x 25½ in) of vintage cloth for the front
65 x 52 cm (25½ x 20½in) and 65 x 37 cm (25½ x 14½in) of vintage cloth for the back
18 cm x 4 m (7in x 4⅜ yd) of vintage cloth for the frill
white thread
pins

1.   Fold the long strip of fabric in half widthways and machine stitch along the short ends with a 1 cm (⅜ in) seam allowance to close into a circle. Press the seam open.

2.   Fold this circle of fabric in half, wrong sides facing, and work long running (gathering) stitches along unfolded edges. Gather to make a 260 cm (102½ in) frill.

3.   Lay the 65 cm (25½ in) fabric square out flat, place the frill on top, lining up the edges. Even out the gathers and tack (baste) using long stitch. For the cushion back, stitch a double hem of 3 cm (1⅛ in) on one of the 65 cm (25½ in) sides of each of the vintage cloth rectangles. Then place the two rectangles on top, the right side of the rectangles against the right side of the square, letting the hemmed sides overlap to form a square (see diagram, top right). Stitch all around with a 1 cm (⅜ in) seam allowance. Trim the excess fabric at the corners.

4.   Turn out the cover and press; slip the cushion pad inside.

PLASTER STATUE

statue
starch
soft brush
toothbrush
paint brush

1.   Begin by mixing equal parts of the starch with water to obtain a fairly thick mixture.

2.   Take the object to be treated and coat it in plaster using the paint brush, paying particular attention to the details and getting into the little recesses. Leave to dry thoroughly.

3.   Once dry, lightly brush; a toothbrush is best for getting into the little recesses.

THE BEDROOM

PATCHWORK QUILT
88

SAMPLER PICTURE
92

FURNITURE RENOVATION
94

DRAWER SACHETS
96

HANGING PLAQUES
98

BOLSTER CUSHIION
100

ROUND CUSHION
102

SMALL TOTE
104

BATH SHEET
106

WASH BAG
108

DUVET COVER
110

SHOULDER BAG
114

PATCHWORK QUILT

134 x 144 cm (52¼ x 56¾ in) of thick fleece on a roll
134 x 144 cm (52¼ x 56¾ in) of floral ticking
different fabrics: plain, printed and linen
textile dye: different shades of blue and grey
lace, braid
5 self-cover buttons, in different sizes
matching thread
pins

1.   Cut out squares and rectangles from the different fabrics. Dye the fabric pieces in the washing machine, mixing the blues and the greys to soften the colours over several loads to obtain a variety of colours. Also dye the ticking and the lace.

2.   Working to the final dimensions of the quilt (134 x 144 cm/52¼ x 56¾ in), and taking inspiration from the diagram overleaf, draw a patchwork pattern with pieces in different sizes. Cut your fabric pieces from the dyed fabrics, adding 1 cm (⅜ in) all around for the seams. Sew strips of lace and braid to some of the pieces.

3.   Join the pieces of fabric together: place two pieces right sides facing matching up along one side, and machine stitch with a 1 cm (⅜ in) seam allowance. Press the seam open. Join all the pieces together in this way to make a rectangle 134 x 144 cm (52¼ x 56¾ in).

4.   Once the patchwork is finished, pin the fleece to the reverse. Then place the ticking on the patchwork, right sides facing, and stitch all three layers together with a 2 cm (¾ in) seam allowance leaving an opening of 30 cm (12 in) on one side. Trim excess fabric at the corners and turn out to the right side. Press, then close the opening by hand using slip stitch.

5.   Cover the buttons with fabric and sew in different places across the quilt, catching in the three thicknesses of the quilt in the sewing.

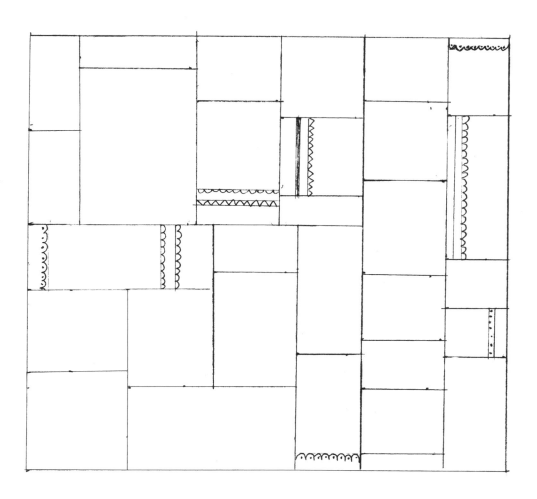

SAMPLER PICTURE

stretcher, 29.5 x 41 cm (11½ x 16⅛ in)
35 x 45 cm (13¾ x 17⅝ in) of blue linen with 12 threads to the centimetre (30 threads to the inch)
4 skeins of DMC stranded cotton (floss), white 5200
stapler

1.   Oversew the edges of the linen and fold into four to mark the centre. Mark the central point of the chart and start the embroidery from here (for chart, see Patterns). Embroider using cross stitch over two threads of weft and two threads of warp with two strands of the thread.

2.   Once the embroidery is complete, stretch the cloth on the stretcher centring the motif. Staple the embroidery to the back of the stretcher.

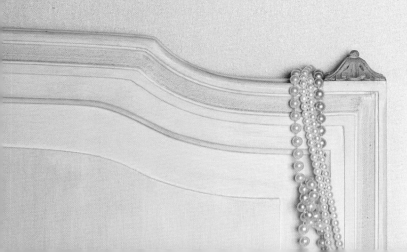

FURNITURE RENOVATION

furniture
fine sandpaper
acrylic paint, matt white and matt beige
white candle
colourless beeswax
sponge
paint brush
fine steel wool

1. One way to bring new life to old furniture is to treat it with a patina finish. First, lightly sand the furniture using the sandpaper and wipe off the dust using a damp sponge.

2. Apply a coat of white paint and leave to dry thoroughly.

3. Rub the edges of the piece of furniture with the candle.

4. Paint the piece of furniture with the beige paint. For an even more aged effect, use two different shades of beige to create the nuances on the doors and drawers.

5. Lightly sand the whole of the piece of furniture so that the white paint shows through. Focus on the areas where the candle was applied to make the edges show through nicely.

6. Wipe away the dust with a damp sponge.

7. Melt the wax in a pan and apply to the whole of the piece of furniture with a clean paint brush. Leave to dry.

8. Rub with fine steel wool to add shine.

DRAWER SACHETS

scraps of denim and different printed cottons
stranded cotton (floss), red
lavender
matching thread
pins

FOR THE HEART

1.   Pin together pieces of denim and printed cotton fabric, right sides facing. Draw the outline of a heart and cut out 1 cm (⅜ in) away from the edge. Unpin.

2.   Cut out a rectangle 5 x 4 cm (2 x 1½ in) and one 4 x 3 cm (1½ in x 1⅛ in) from the scraps of printed cotton and press a 5 mm (¼ in) hem all around. Pin the rectangles onto the denim heart and sew with two strands of embroidery thread, using straight stitch and running stitch.

3.   Place the hearts one on top of the other, right sides facing, and stitch all around with a 1 cm (⅜ in) seam allowance, leaving an opening of 5 cm (2 in) on one side. Cut notches into the curves and at the tip of the heart.

4.   Turn right side out and press. Fill with lavender by making a little cone with a sheet of paper. Close up the opening using slip stitch.

FOR THE SQUARE

1.   Cut out four squares 9 x 9 cm (3½ x 3½ in) from the different fabrics for the front and one 16 x 16 cm (6¼ x 6¼in) for the back.

2.   Join together two small squares by stitching along one side with a 1 cm (⅜ in) seam allowance; press the seam open. Do the same with the other two squares. Then join the joined squares together to give you a large square 16 cm x 16 cm (6¼ x 6¼in). Trim the seams and press flat.

3.   Position the two large squares right sides facing and stitch all around leaving an opening of 5 cm (2 in). Cut notches at the corners, then turn right side out. Fill with lavender and close using slip stitch.

HANGING PLAQUES

self-hardening modelling clay, white
lace and stamps, etc., for stamping clay
round vessels in different diameters (glasses, bowls, cups, tins, etc.)
acrylic paint, cream
satin varnish
rolling pin
craft knife
fine paint brush

1.   Work the clay, then roll it out using the rolling pin to make a plaque around 3mm (⅛ in) thick. Imprint the top of the clay using stamps and any other objects that you wish (for the lace, you'll need to press it down firmly into the clay using the rolling pin to mark the design clearly, then carefully remove).

2.   Use the round vessel to mark circles out onto the printed clay; cut out the circles using the pointed blade of the craft knife. Turn up the edges all around by pinching the clay between two fingers and smoothing the edge by moistening slightly. Leave to dry for the recommended time.

3.   Paint the motifs using the acrylic paint in cream, varnish some areas to obtain different nuances of white and texture.

4.   Use a strong adhesive to stick a length of ribbon to the back of the plaques for hanging.

BOLSTER CUSHION

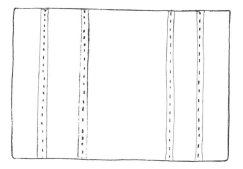

48 x 54 cm (19 x 21¼ in) of white linen or cotton fabric
2 circles 18 cm (7 in) in diameter of white linen or cotton fabric
2 strips 10 x 54 cm (4 x 21¼ in) of blue linen fabric
10 x 54 cm (4 x 21¼ in) of printed fabric
14 x 54 cm (5½ x 21¼ in) of fabric in another matching print
30 x 54 cm (12 x 21¼ in) of another printed fabric
4 strips of lace 54 cm (21¼ in)
2 large self-cover buttons
scraps of fabric for the buttons
wadding (batting)
matching thread
pins

1.   For the bolster pad, fold the white linen in half to give you a rectangle measuring 27 x 48 cm (10½ x 19in). Machine stitch the long edge with a 1 cm (⅜ in) seam allowance to make a tube, leaving an opening of 20 cm (8 in) in the middle. Pin the two circles to the ends and stitch with a 1 cm (⅜ in) seam allowance. Cut notches and turn out through the opening. Press, fill with wadding (batting) and close using slip stitch.

2.   For the bolster cover, join the different strips together (along the 54 cm/21¼ in side), placing them right sides facing and stitching with a 1 cm (⅜ in) seam allowance: start with the two strips in matching prints 10 cm (4 in) and 14 cm (5½ in) wide, then join together the 30 cm (12 in) printed strip and then the two 10 cm (4 in) blue strips. Press open all the seams and stitch a strip of lace over each seam.

3.   Stitch a 1 cm (⅜ in) hem at each end of the strip. Fold in half lengthways, right sides facing, and stitch with a 1 cm (⅜ in) seam allowance. Press the seam open, turn out to the right side and work a line of long running (gathering) stitches around each opening.

4.   Slip the bolster pad inside the cover and pull on the gathering threads to close the ends. Cover the two buttons with fabric and sew them onto each end.

ROUND CUSHION

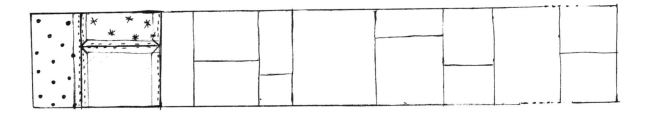

1 circle of white woollen cloth 19 cm (17½ in) in diameter
1 circle 13 cm (5 in) in diameter cut out of a napkin or a monogrammed sheet
scraps of printed cotton in shades of blue and grey
45 cm (17⅝ in) of scalloped edging
wadding (batting)
matching thread
pins

1.   With the scraps of cotton, make a strip of patchwork 115 x 13 cm (45¼ x 5in), taking inspiration from the sketch above. Cut out the squares and rectangles in different sizes, remembering to add 1 cm (⅜ in) all around for the seam allowance. Join them together by placing one piece on top of another, right sides facing, lining up one of the sides, and sewing with a 1 cm (⅜ in) seam allowance; press the seam open. Join together all the pieces in this way, trimming excess fabric at the corners to avoid excess thickness.

2.   Fold the patchwork strip in half, right sides facing and lining up along the two short edges. Stitch together with a 1 cm (⅜ in) seam allowance to join into a circle. Pin the joined patchwork strip onto the circle of woollen cloth, lining up the edges, right sides facing. Stitch together with a 1 cm (⅜ in) seam allowance then cut notches all around.

3.   Turn right side out and press. Work a line of long running (gathering) stitches around the opening. Fill the cushion with wadding (batting) and pull up the threads to gather; tie off securely.

4.   Make a scalloped edging to the monogrammed circle by machine, using satin stitch. Pin the scalloped edging all around on the reverse of this circle, then sew the circle to the centre of the cushion using blind stitch to close the opening, catching the scalloped edging in the seam.

SMALL TOTE

2 rectangles 30 x 27 cm (12 x 10½ in) of woollen cloth dyed grey for the bag
2 rectangles 30 x 15 cm (12 x 5¾ in) of woollen cloth dyed blue for the bag
2 rectangles 40 x 30 cm (15⅝ x 12 in) of woollen cloth dyed grey for the lining
2 strips 28 x 8 cm (11 x 3⅛ in) of woollen cloth dyed blue for the handles
1 rectangle of woollen cloth with monogram, 20 x 15 cm (8 x 5¾ in)
70 cm (27½ in) of scalloped edging
3 strips of different lace 60 cm (23½ in) long
matching thread
pins

1. Starting with the bag fabric, pin a rectangle of grey woollen cloth with a rectangle of blue woollen cloth, lining up the 30 cm (12 in) side, and stitch together with a 1 cm (⅜ in) seam allowance. Repeat for the other two rectangles. Press open the seams.

2. Make a 5 mm (¼ in) hem on the reverse of the monogram, and pin it to the centre of the 28 x 8 cm (11 x 3⅛ in) piece of grey fabric. Sew the monogram using long stitch and stitch the scalloped edging by machine all around.

3. Pin the back and the front of the bag, right sides facing, ensuring that the grey and blue fabrics line up. Stitch along the sides and the bottom with a 1 cm (⅜ in) seam allowance and trim the excess fabric at the corners.

4. Join together the lining fabric in the same way, leaving an opening at the bottom of around 12 cm (4¾ in).

5. Fold the fabric strips for the handles in half and stitch along the length with a 1 cm (⅜ in) seam allowance. Turn out and press. Pin the handles, lining up the edges with the opening of the bag, onto the right side, 7 cm (2¾ in) from each side.

6. Slip the bag into its lining, right sides facing, and stitch all around the opening with a 1 cm (⅜ in) seam allowance. Turn right side out through the opening left in the lining and then close up using slip stitch. Push the lining back inside the bag and press well.

7. Pin the strips of lace around the top of the bag following the photograph, and sew on by hand.

BATH SHEET

84 x 150 cm (33 x 60 in) of vintage woollen cloth dyed blue
44 x 82.5 cm (17¼ x 32½ in) of printed fabric
2 pieces of lace, 80 cm (31½ in)
tracing paper
matching threads
pins

1.   Fold a double hem of 2 cm (¾ in) along one short and the two long sides of the piece of woollen cloth, trimming off excess fabric at the corners; machine stitch.

2.   Photocopy the template for the bath sheet enlarging by 120% and trace (see Patterns). Fold the printed fabric in half, right sides facing, to give you a rectangle measuring 22 x 82.5 cm (8⅝ x 32½ in). Transfer the template repeating it along the length of the strip, placing the rounded edges along the fold.

3.   Stitch along the sides and the rounded edges of the printed fabric with a 1 cm (⅜ in) seam allowance. Cut notches into the curves and trim the excess fabric at the corners. Turn out the fabric onto the right side and press flat.

4.   Fold up a 1 cm (⅜ in) hem along the unscallopped edges of the edging, slip the blue fabric inside and pin. Stitch 2 mm (³⁄₃₂ in) from the edge.

5.   Pin two strips of lace, one above the other, level with the seam at the bottom of the edging, and stitch in place.

WASH BAG

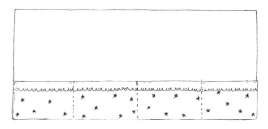

63 x 35 cm (24¾ x 13¾ in) of vintage linen
1 circle of vintage linen 20 cm (8 in) in diameter for the base
63 x 13 cm (24¾ x 5 in) of printed fabric
63 cm (24¾ in) of scalloped braid
1 m (39¼ in) of satin ribbon 1 cm (⅜ in) wide
stitch unpicker
safety pin
matching thread
pins

1. Oversew all the pieces of fabric. Pin the scalloped braid to one of the lengths of the printed fabric, wrong sides facing, and stitch with a 1 cm (⅜ in) seam allowance. Turn out the scalloped border and press flat (see diagram).

2. Pin the printed fabric onto the large rectangle of linen, with the wrong side of the printed fabric to the right side of the linen, lining up the edges. Sew a line of stitching vertically onto the printed fabric, approximately every 15 cm (5¾ in), to make the pockets.

3. Fold the linen, right sides facing, and stitch together to make a tube. Pin the base to the bottom of the bag, right sides facing, and stitch with a 1 cm (⅜ in) seam allowance. Press.

4. Press a double turn-up of 1 cm (⅜ in) at the top of the bag, and make another 5 cm (2 in) turn-up. First stitch along the edge of the double turn-up to hold it in place, then make a second row of stitches 2 cm (¾ in) from the first and a third 2 cm (¾ in) above to make the channel for the ribbon drawstring. Turn out, open the vertical seam (using the stitch unpicker) between the first two horizontal seams, so that you can thread through the ribbon with the help of a safety pin.

DUVET COVER

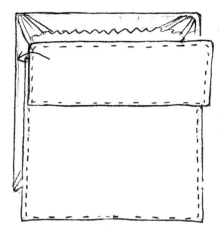

FOR A DUVET 240 x 220 cm (94½ x 86½ in)
2 remnants of white woollen cloth, 242 x 222 cm (95¼ x 87½ in)

FOR TWO PILLOW CASES
4 squares of white woollen cloth, 64 x 64 cm (25 x 25 in)
2 rectangles of white woollen cloth, 26 x 64 cm (10⅛ x 25 in)
20.5 m (22½ yd) of scalloped edging 10 cm (4 in) wide
scraps of printed fabric
scraps of fine iron-on interfacing
strands of stranded cotton (floss) in different shades of blue-grey
white thread
pins

1.   Line the printed fabrics with iron-on interfacing and cut out small squares and rectangles from them. Pin onto one of the panels of the duvet cover, overlapping some of them, and sew using running stitch with two strands of embroidery thread. On the same panel and on the front of the pillow cases, embroider the repeat motifs with two strands of embroidery thread taking inspiration from the diagrams provided in the Patterns section.

2.   Pin the edging onto the embroidered panel of the duvet, right sides facing and lining up the edges, starting at the bottom. At the corners, pleat 50 cm (20 in) of edging and spread these folds out starting 10 cm (4 in) before the corners and finishing 10 cm (4 in) after. To finish, overlap the edging by 2 cm (¾ in). Place the second panel on top, pin and stitch with a 1 cm (⅜ in) seam allowance, leaving an opening of 50 cm (20 in) in the middle at the bottom of the duvet. At the opening, hem the underneath panel and stitch the edging to the top panel. Trim excess fabric at the corners, turn out and press.

3.   Embroider the pillow cases in the same way as the duvet. Stitch a double hem of 1 cm (⅜ in) on two of the squares and on the two rectangles. Pin the scalloped edging on the embroidered top of one pillow case, right sides facing and lining up the edges. Place over the hemmed square and the rectangle, matching up their hemmed sides so that they form a square 64 x 64 cm (25 x 25 in) as in the diagram above. Stitch all around the edges, trim off excess fabric at the corners and turn out.

SHOULDER BAG

2 rectangles 19 x 25 cm (7½ x 9⅞in) of striped fabric

2 rectangles 19 x 25 cm (7½ x 9⅞in) of floral fabric

36 x 30 cm (12 in) of ecru cotton/linen fabric

141 x 6 cm (55½ x 2⅜ in) and 64 x 6 cm (25 x 2⅜ in) of ecru cotton/linen fabric

8 cm (3⅛ in) of fine ribbon

1 self-cover button, 30 mm in diameter

a scrap of printed fabric

34 cm (13⅜ in) of lace for the bag flap

17 cm (6¾ in) of lace for the bottom of the bag

pattern paper

matching thread

pins

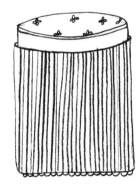

1.   Place the two rectangles of floral fabric right sides facing and machine stitch along the sides and the bottom with a 1 cm (⅜ in) seam allowance. Do the same for the striped fabric, placing the 17 cm (6¾ in) length of lace at the bottom between the two thicknesses of fabric (but not right up to the edge of the fabric, so that it overhangs nicely when the bag is turned out). Press open the seams.

2.   Turn out the striped bag, and slip the floral lining inside, wrong sides facing. Fold over 1 cm (⅜ in) at the top of the floral fabric and the striped fabric, and press to mark the creases.

3.   Fold the large piece of ecru cotton/linen fabric in half, right sides facing, to give you a rectangle measuring 36 x 15 cm (14⅛ x 5¾ in). Photocopy the flap template (see Patterns), transfer onto the pattern paper and then onto the fabric. Cut out to give you two flaps.

4.   Place the front and the reverse of the flap together, right sides facing. Place the lace between the two pieces of fabric along the rounded edge (but not right up to the edge of the fabric, so that it overhangs when the flap is turned out). Place the ribbon, folded in half, in the middle of the flap, as in the diagram, below right; pin. Stitch all along the rounded edge with a 1 cm (⅜ in) seam allowance ensuring that the lace is caught in the seam. Cut notches, turn out and press.

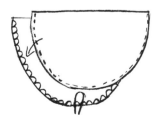

5.   Fold the two strips of cotton/linen fabric in half lengthways and stitch with a 1 cm (⅜ in) seam allowance. To turn out, pin a safety pin onto one end of the strip, slip inside and bring out the other end; press. Hem one of the ends of each strip; slip the unhemmed end between the bag and its lining so that it is level with the side seams, inserting it by 1 cm (⅜ in). Slip the flap in between the bag and the lining at the back and pin in place. Stitch all around the top of the bag 5 mm (¼ in) from the edge. Cover the button with fabric and sew onto the front of the bag to line up with the ribbon loop. Tie the two parts of the strap into a pretty bow.

PATTERNS

APRON
120
PENCIL CASE
121
KEY HOLDER
122
WOOL BASKET
122
CHAIR COVER
123
FABRIC FRUIT & VEGETABLES
124
HANGING ORNAMENT
125
COVERED NOTEBOOKS
126–127
TABLECLOTH & NAPKINS
128–129
ARMCHAIR RENOVATION
130–133
SAMPLER PICTURE
134–135
BATH SHEET
136
DUVET COVER
137
SHOULDER BAG
138
BLACKBOARD
139

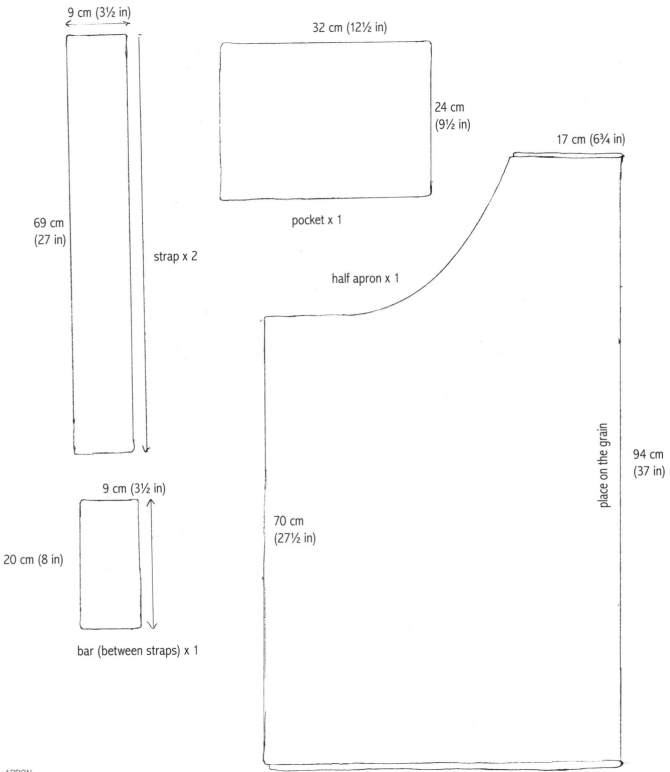

9 cm (3½ in)

69 cm
(27 in)

strap x 2

32 cm (12½ in)

24 cm
(9½ in)

pocket x 1

17 cm (6¾ in)

half apron x 1

place on the grain

94 cm
(37 in)

9 cm (3½ in)

20 cm (8 in)

bar (between straps) x 1

70 cm
(27½ in)

PENCIL CASE

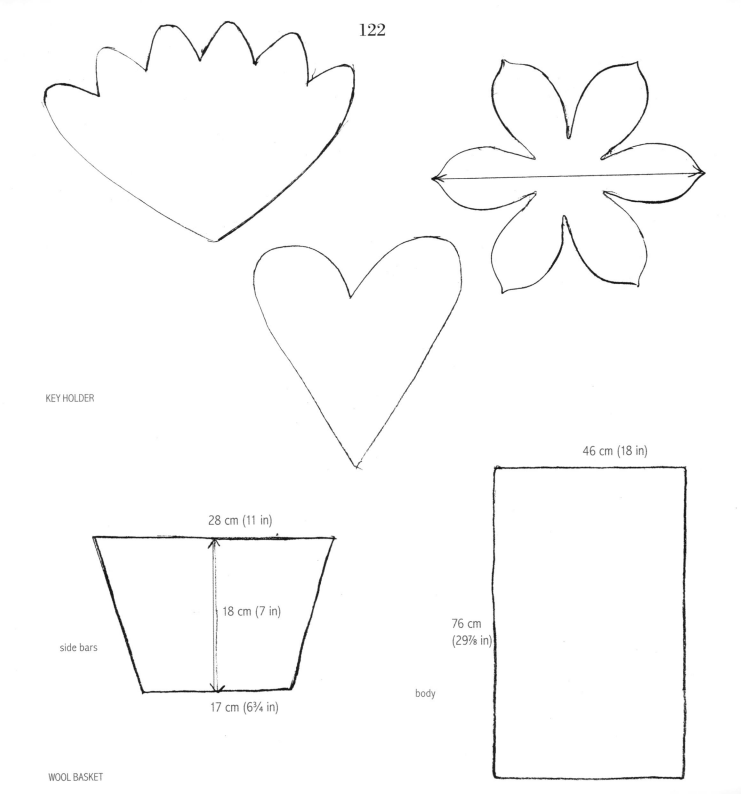

KEY HOLDER

28 cm (11 in)

18 cm (7 in)

side bars

17 cm (6¾ in)

WOOL BASKET

46 cm (18 in)

76 cm
(29⅞ in)

body

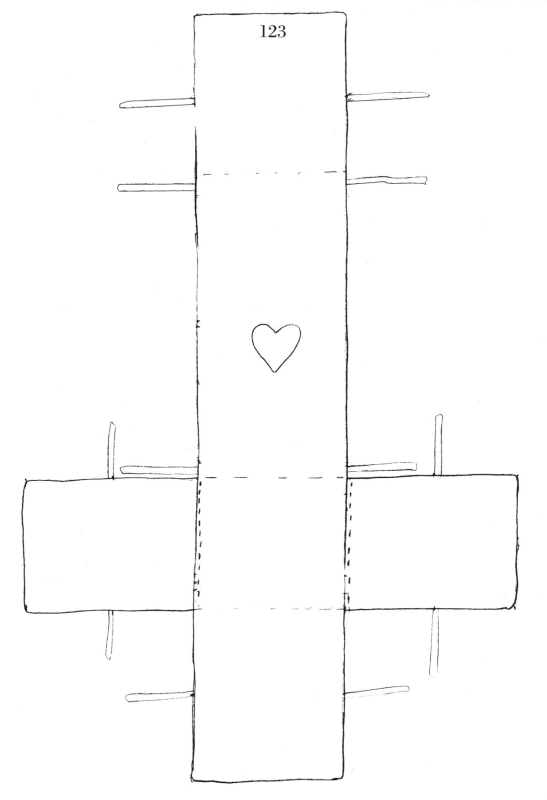

123

CHAIR COVER

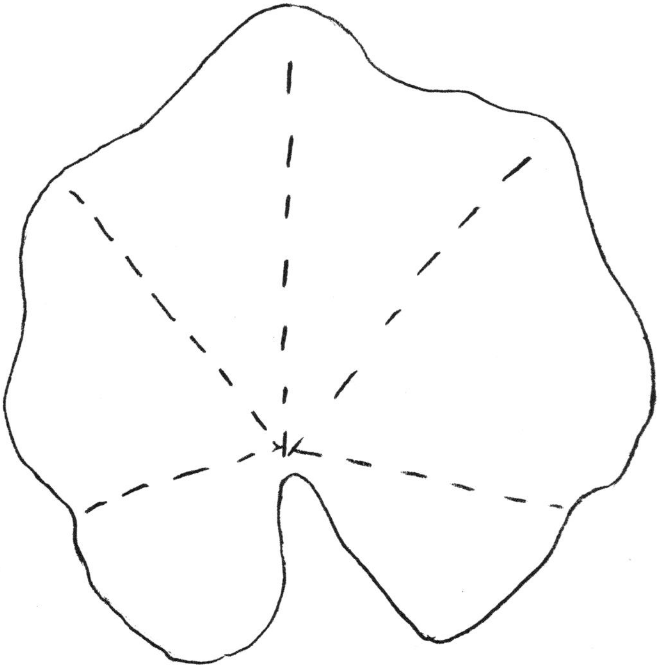

pumpkin stem x 2

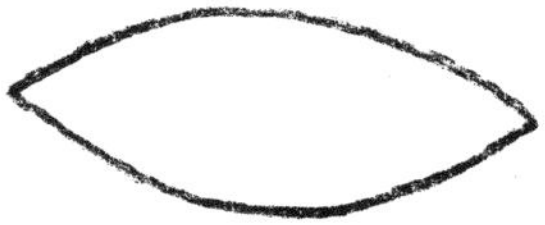

pear leaf x 2

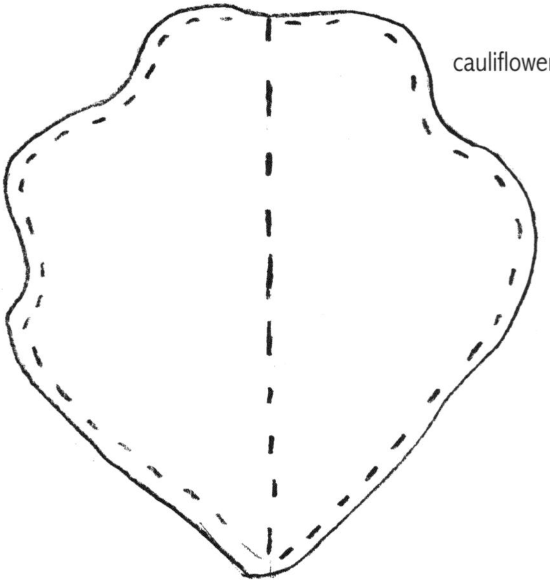

pumpkin leaf x 1

cauliflower leaf x 5

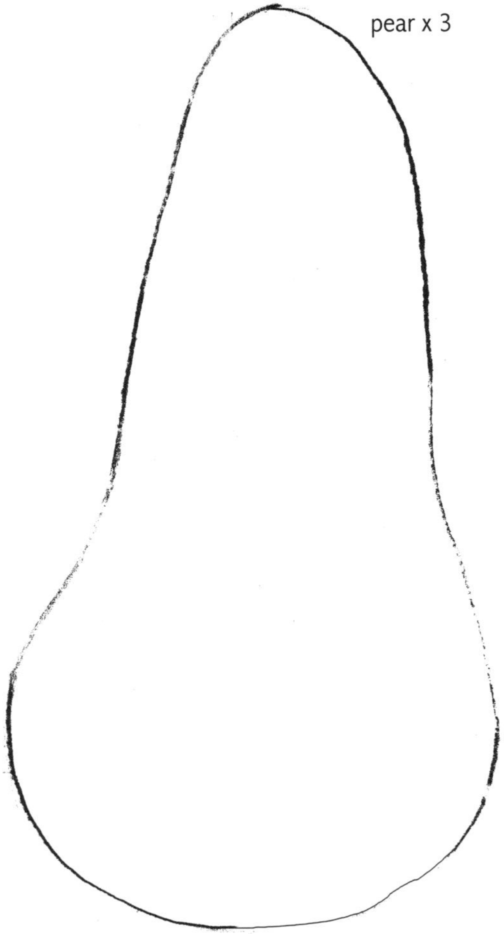

pear x 3

bird

HANGING ORNAMENT

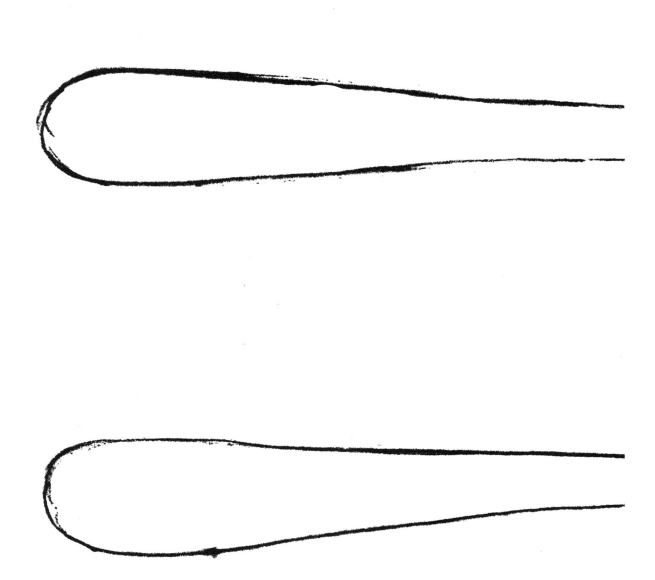

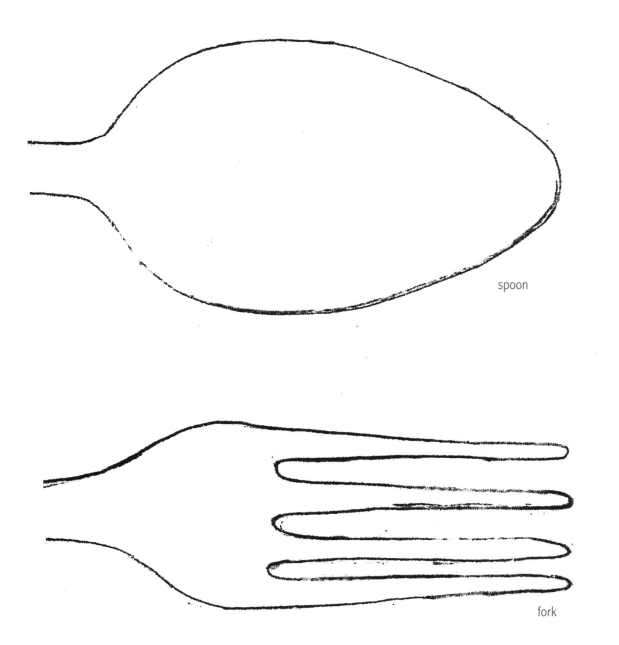

spoon

fork

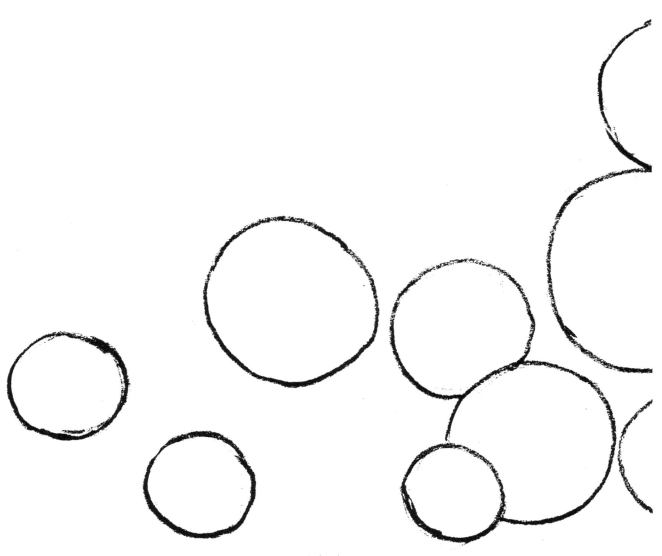

circle placement

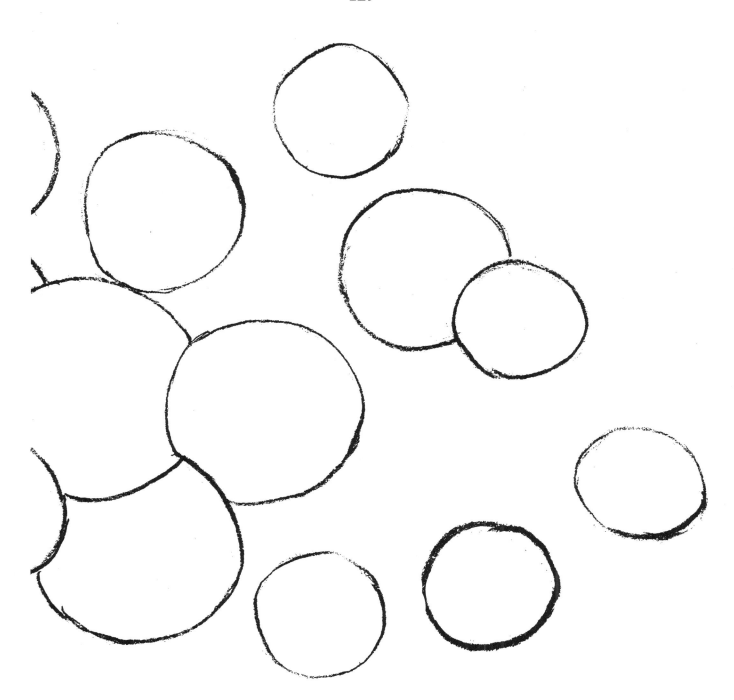

cut 1

cut 1

cut 1

cut 2

cut 2

cut 2

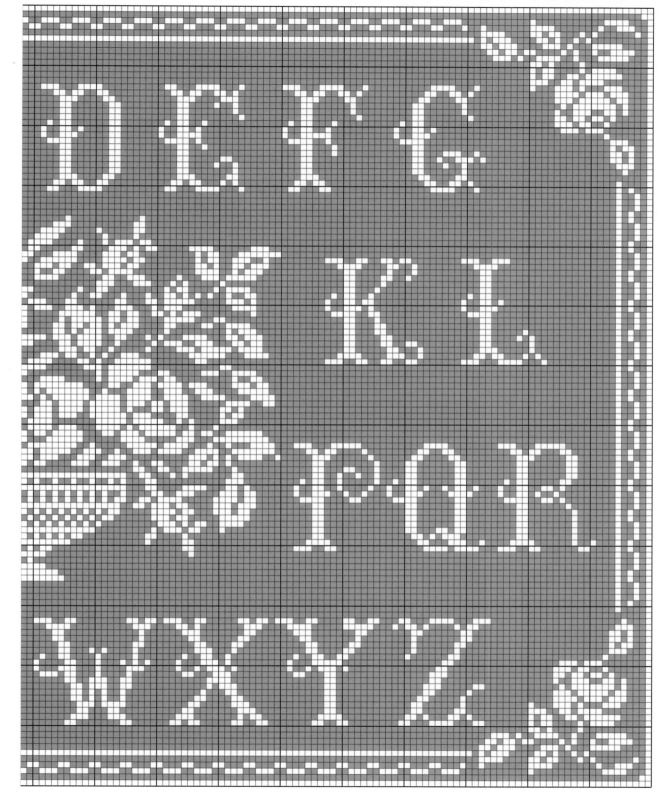

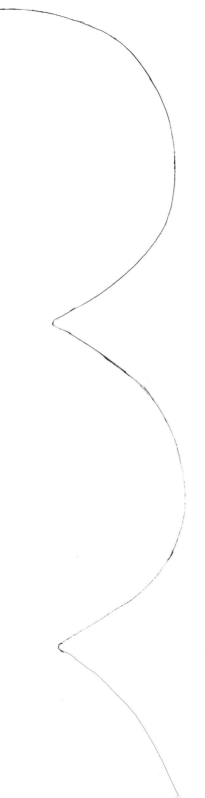

edging

BATH SHEET enlarge by 120%

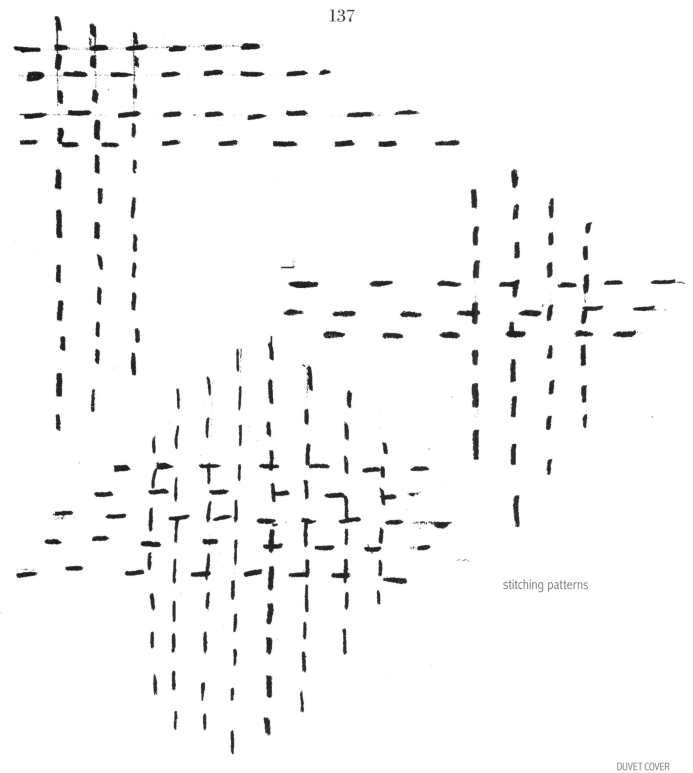

stitching patterns

DUVET COVER

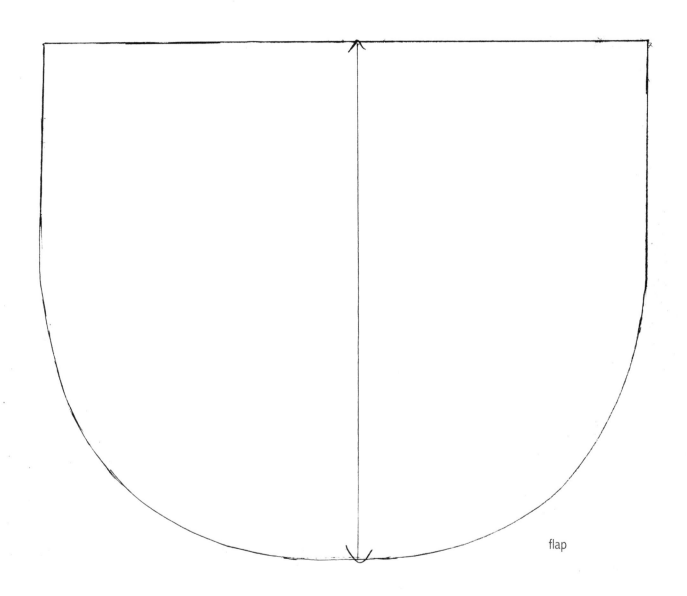

flap

SHOULDER BAG

BLACKBOARD enlarge by 200%

DIRECTORY

UK

Panduro Hobby
Westway House
Transport Avenue
Brentford
Middlesex
TW8 9HF
Tel: 020 8566 1680
trade@panduro.co.uk
www.pandurohobby.co.uk

Coast and Country Crafts & Quilts
8 Sampson Gardens
Ponsanooth
Truro
Cornwall
TR3 7RS
Tel: 01872 863894
www.coastandcountrycrafts.co.uk

Threads and Patches
48 Aylesbury Street
Fenny Stratford
Bletchley
Milton Keynes
MK2 2BU
Tel: 01908 649687
www.threadsandpatches.co.uk

The Cotton Patch
1283-1285 Stratford Road
Hall Green
Birmingham
B28 9AJ
Tel: 0121 702 2840
www.cottonpatch.co.uk

Puddlecrafts
3 Milltown Lodge
Sandpit
Termonfeckin
County Louth
Ireland
Tel: 00353 87 355 0219
www.puddlecrafts.co.uk

The Fat Quarters
5 Choprell Road
Blackhall Mill
Newcastle
NE17 7TN
Tel: 01207 565728
www.thefatquarters.co.uk

Fred Aldous Ltd.
37 Lever Street
Manchester
M1 1LW
Tel: 08707 517301
www.fredaldous.co.uk

The Sewing Bee
52 Hillfoot Street
Dunoon
Argyll
PA23 7DT
Tel: 01369 706879
www.thesewingbee.co.uk

The Eternal Maker
89 Oving Road
Chichester
West Sussex
PO19 7EW
www.eternalmaker.com

Loop Fabrics
32 West Hill Road
Brighton
BN1 3RT
www.loopfabric.co.uk

Whaleys
Harris Court
Great Horton
Bradford
BD7 4EQ
www.whaleys-bradford.ltd.uk

USA

Coats and Clark USA
PO Box 12229
Greenville
SC29612-0229
Tel: 1 800 648 1479
www.coatsandclark.com

Keepsake Quilting
Box 1618
Center Harbor
NH 03226
Tel: 1 800 525 8086
www.keepsakequilting.com

The City Quilter
157 West 24th Street
New York
NY 1011
Tel: 1 212 807 0390
www.cityquilter.com

Connecting Threads
13118 NE 4th Street
Vancouver
WA 9884
Tel: 1 800 574 6454
www.connectingthreads.com

The Craft Connection
21055 Front Street
PO Box 1088
Onley
VA 23418
Tel: 1 888 204 4050
www.craftconn.com

eQuilter
545 Spine Road
Suite E
Boulder
CO 80301
Tel: 1 877 322 7423
www.equilter.com

Hamels Fabrics
5843 Lickman Road
Chilliwack
British Columbia
V2R 4B5
Tel: 1 877 774 2635
www.hamelsfabrics.com

JoAnn Stores Inc.
55 Darrow Road
Hudson
OH 44236
Tel: 1 888 739 4120
www.joann.com

Pink Chalk Fabrics
9723 Coppertop Loop
Suite 205
Bainbridge Island
WA 98110
Tel: 1 888 894 0658
www.pinkchalkfabrics.com

J&O Fabrics
9401 Rt.130
Pennsauken
NJ 08110
www.jandofabrics.com

Purl Soho
459 Broome Street
New York
NY 10013
www.purlsoho.com

INDEX

Apron 10--13, 120
Armchair Renovation 76--7, 130--3

bags
    Drawstring Bag 34--7
    Large Tote 60--1
    Shoulder Bag 114--15, 138
    Small Tote 104--5
    Wash Bag 108--9
Bath Sheet 106--7, 136
Bedroom projects 87--117
    Bath Sheet 106--7, 136
    Bolster Cushion 100--1
    Drawer Sachet Cushions 96--7
    Duvet Cover 110--13, 137
    Furniture Renovation 94--5
    Hanging Plaques 98--9
    Patchwork Quilt 88--91
    Round Cushion 102--3
    Sampler Picture 92--3, 134--5
    Shoulder Bag 114--15, 138
    Small Tote 104--5
    Wash Bag 108--9
bird designs, Hanging Ornament 74--5, 125
Blackboard 38--9, 139
Bolster Cushion 100--1
Boxes, Covered 16--19
Bread Basket 62--3

chairs, projects for
    Armchair Renovation 76--7, 130--3
    Chair Cover 46--7, 123
    Seat Pad 14--15
Cotton Reel Holder 20--1
Covered Boxes 16--19
cushions
    Bolster Cushion 100--1
    Drawer Sachet Cushions 96--7
    Floor Cushion 80--1

Heart Cushion 72--3
Rectangular Cushion 78--9
Round Cushion 102--3
Seat Pad 14--15

Display Board 52--3
Drawer Sachet Cushions 96--7
Drawstring Bag 34--7
Duvet Cover 110--13, 137

Fabric Fruit & Vegetables 48--51, 124
Floor Cushion 80--1
Fruit & Vegetables, Fabric 48--51, 124
furniture
    Furniture Renovation 94--5
    see also chairs, projects for

Hanging Ornament 74--5, 125
Hanging Plaques 98--9
heart designs
    Drawer Sachet Cushions 96--7
    Heart Cushion 72--3

Jar Labels 40--1

Key Holder 30--1

Labels, Jar 40--1
Lamp Shade 54--5
Large Tote 60--1

Napkins 68--71, 128--9
Needle Roll 24--5
Notebook Covers 64--7, 126--7

Patchwork Quilt 88--91
patina finish 94--5
patterns 119--39
Pencil Case 22--3, 121

Picture Sampler 92--3, 134--5
pillow cases 110--13
Pin Cushion 32--3
Plant Pot Covers 56--9
Plaster Statue 82--3

Quilt, Patchwork 88--91

Rectangular Cushion 78--9
Round Cushion 102--3

Sampler Picture 92--3, 134--5
Seat Pad 14--15
Shoulder Bag 114--15, 138
Sitting Room projects 45--85
    Armchair Renovation 76--7, 130--3
    Bread Basket 62--3
    Chair Cover 46--7, 123
    Display Board 52--3
    Fabric Fruit & Vegetables 48--51, 124
    Floor Cushion 80--1
    Hanging Ornament 74--5, 125
    Heart Cushion 72--3
    Lamp Shade 54--5
    Large Tote 60--1
    Notebook Covers 64--7, 126--7
    Plant Pot Covers 56--9
    Plaster Statue 82--3
    Rectangular Cushion 78--9
    Tablecloth 68--71, 128--9
Small Tote 104--5
Statue, Plaster 82--3

Tablecloth 68--71, 128--9
towels, Bath Sheet 106--7, 136

Vegetables, Fabric 48--51, 124

Wash Bag 108--9

Wool Basket 26--9, 122
Workshop projects 9--43
    Apron 10--13, 120
    Blackboard 38--9, 139
    Cotton Reel Holder 20--1
    Covered Boxes 16--19
    Drawstring Bag 34--7
    Jar Labels 40--1
    Key Holder 30--1
    Needle Roll 24--5
    Pencil Case 22--3, 121
    Pin Cushion 32--3
    Seat Pad 14--15
    Wool Basket 26--9, 122

ACKNOWLEDGEMENTS

With thanks to V. for all those things that words can't express,

With thanks to Camille and Dora for being so patient with a mum who wasn't always available,

With thanks to Pascale for believing in me. Thank you for listening, for your patience and also for your enthusiasm and encouragement that was so precious to me,

With thanks to Lélia and Frédéric for their beautiful pictures and for putting their hearts into this project.

Thanks for bringing it so beautifully to life,

With thanks to Agnès for her marvellous embroidery,

With thanks to Christine for her delicate work,

With thanks to Dominique for her accurate proofing,

With thanks to my beautiful Isabelle for her help, thanks for being there, always,

With thanks to Catherine and Jean-Paul, without whom I couldn't have done it!

With thanks to my little Vania for being who she is, I'm looking forward to a new project!

With thanks to Françoise and Antoinette for their help and their magic touch,

A big thank you to Franck and Isabelle for the warm welcome they gave us in their home,

With thanks to all those I don't know who worked on this project,

With thanks to my family and friends, who support me and continually encourage me.